POEMS OF THE PASSING

Rúhíyyih Rabbani

POEMS OF THE PASSING

BY

RÚHÍYYIH RABBANI

GEORGE RONALD
OXFORD

George Ronald, Publisher
46 High Street, Kidlington, Oxford OX5 2DN

© Rúhíyyih Rabbani 1996

All Rights Reserved

A cataloguing in Publication Number
is available from the British Library

ISBN 0–85398–410–7

Printed and bound in Great Britain by
Biddles Ltd, Guildford and King's Lynn

CONTENTS

Introduction

Rúḥíyyih Rabbani is the widow of Shoghi Effendi Rabbani, great-grandson of Bahá'u'lláh, the prophetic nineteenth century figure whose vision of global unity is becoming increasingly relevant to the direction of contemporary history. As head for thirty-six years (1921–1957) of the Bahá'í movement, Shoghi Effendi devoted himself to giving practical expression to Bahá'u'lláh's ideals.[1] In this effort he was brilliantly successful. Today, embracing people from more than 2,100 ethnic, racial and tribal groups, and established in the most remote corners of the earth, the community he inspired and shaped represents the most diverse organized body of people on the planet. Its unity and achievements pose searching challenges for materialistic theories of human nature.

Neither the scale nor the diversity of the expansion, however, adequately conveys the creative genius that achieved it. Faced with the need to inspire in the small, widely-scattered, and heterogenous body of Bahá'u'lláh's followers in various countries the passion and the sense of common purpose needed for their enormous task, Shoghi Effendi found in himself a range of talents and resources whose rapid cultivation is breathtaking to contemplate. His life offers an instance of that phenomenon—rare indeed in the twentieth century—for which an earlier age coined the term "*uomo universale*". Any one of the major pursuits that occupied his thirty-six years at the helm of Bahá'í activities would have distinguished the lifetime achievements of most professional careers. Driven by the historic imperative he found in Bahá'u'lláh's perception that contemporary civilization is breaking apart, Shoghi Effendi made of himself variously an author, an administrator, a historian, an inspired translator (from Arabic and Persian to English and the reverse), a daring patron of architecture, a trenchant analyst of world trends, and a master planner able to conceive in his mind the components of undertakings whose scope of operations was the entire planet.

Somehow, this awesome array of occupations left time for unhurried hours of informal conversations over the dinner table with a constant stream of collaborators and admirers drawn from all over the world to the international centre of his work at Haifa. Hundreds of written accounts speak of the impact of a personality that made the evenings spent at his table among the most memorable experiences of his guests' lives.

During the summer months, temporarily released from the demands of his labours at home, Shoghi Effendi retired to Switzerland and to the mountain climbing that brought him peace and time for reflection.

On 24 March 1937, he married Mary Sutherland Maxwell, daughter of a prominent Montreal family. Partly because of her mother's ill health and partly because of the independent nature of her own mind, Mary's education was largely supplied by a succession of private tutors. Gifted with great energy and an intensely inquiring mind, she supplemented this basic curriculum with an eclectic range of studies that included subjects as diverse as economics, literature and German. Family bonds were unusually close, with the result that Mary was powerfully influenced by both the spirit of tolerance and universality that animated her mother and the creativity of her father, William Sutherland Maxwell, one of Canada's premier architects and a perceptive collector of art, antiques and books.

This stimulating and relatively sheltered life ended abruptly with her marriage. In the 1930s, Palestine was still under the British Mandate, and Shoghi Effendi, the hereditary successor of the Founder of the Bahá'í Faith, was viewed in local circles as a highly respected dignitary. Because the teachings of Bahá'u'lláh, his great-grandfather, had attracted violent outbursts of religious persecution from fundamentalist Muslim circles throughout both the Near and Middle East, he was forced to act with great circumspection. It is difficult for a contemporary reader to appreciate the onerous restrictions that the circumstances of this totally new environment imposed upon a young North American bride of cultivated tastes, liberal sympathies, and an eagerness to put her capacities at the service of ideals to which she was totally committed.

That she succeeded appears to have been the result of both her faith in the eventual triumph of these ideals and a marriage that compensated her for all the sacrifices and hardships it brought with it. She became her husband's confidential secretary and indefatigable assistant, answering his vast international correspondence, entertaining an unending succession of guests from every part of the world, and helping with the practical management of the Bahá'í international centre.

She travelled with him, not only to the Swiss mountains, but also to London and Paris where furnishings could be purchased for the historical restorations that were an important part of Shoghi Effendi's work in embellishing the buildings and Archives at the Bahá'í Faith's World Centre in Haifa and 'Akká. Her feeling for buildings and antiques, inherited from her father and her home background, enabled her to be of special help to her illustrious husband in furnishing Bahá'í Holy Places in Haifa and 'Akká. In one of the tributes he paid her, Shoghi Effendi spoke of his wife as "my shield, . . . my tireless collaborator". He gave her the name "Rúḥíyyih", a derivative of the word "spirit", and it is by this name, together with its accompanying honorific "Khánum", that she is best known to the followers of Bahá'u'lláh around the world.

Shoghi Effendi's culminating and most ambitious plan, a ten-year-long program of development, with objectives in over 249 countries and territories, had been only half-way completed by November 1957 when the tragedy of his sudden death produced these heart-broken outpourings in verse, "Poems of the Passing". On the morning of November 4th Rúḥíyyih Khánum entered his room to find that he had died in his sleep from the effects of Asiatic flu. She spoke of the experience in a study of his life and work which she wrote some years after the event:

> Many times people have asked me if I did not notice indications that the end was near. My answer is a hesitant no. If a terrible storm comes suddenly into the midst of a perfect day one can later imagine one saw straws floating by on the wind and pretend they had been portents. . . . I could never have survived the slightest foreknowledge of [his] death, and only survived it in the end because I could not abandon him and his precious work . . .[2]

For the army of people around the world who loved him and devoted their lives to supporting his outstanding leadership, Shoghi Effendi was a unique person. His qualities of heart and mind, his leading role in promoting the plans upon which they were all engaged, his unique vision, made his death an irreparable loss to the Bahá'ís all over the world. In the case of Rúḥíyyih Khánum, the bereavement suffered was at once that of a woman deprived of her husband whom she loved and served and the Head of her Faith.

The poems reproduced here were, for the most part, written during the months that followed Shoghi Effendi's death. They remained, however, in the private papers of their author. The reason can be inferred from the brief passage just quoted from her later study of his life. Neither she nor any of Shoghi Effendi's other co-workers could abandon his lifelong work. By 1963, the ambitious world-wide plans that had seemed imperilled by his death in 1957 had been triumphantly accomplished and, to any objective observer, it was clear that the cause to which Shoghi Effendi had devoted his life was now established on an enduring and self-renewing foundation.

This victory—motivated by Shoghi Effendi's own plans—has brought Bahá'u'lláh's message of global unity within the reach of most of the earth's inhabitants and created a social experiment that argues persuasively for the capacity of human beings from every background to work together as a single people, with the world as their common homeland. The leading figure in this continuing drama has been Rúḥíyyih Khánum herself. Now, over 80 years of age, she has visited some 185 countries and major dependencies.

Her poems, now published for the first time, do not follow the conventional pattern of the literature of mourning: denial, struggle, and a resolution that comes through the acceptance of loss. Rather, her own great tragedy when, in 1957, Shoghi Effendi passed away, called forth from his wife a passionate resolve to ensure the triumph of his work and his plans. Clearly, this effort was animated by a belief in God that appears intermittently throughout these pages like an attenuated, unifying thread, and that finally survived the agony of her parting from her beloved Guardian.

In the poems we overhear an intimate dialogue between the human heart and the soul as they grapple with the existential questions posed by death and loss. Sometimes taut with metaphysical conceptions, sometimes resonant with spontaneous grief, these lyric outpourings embody the soul's quest to know the meaning of "the world", "eternity", "oblivion" ("What Is Time and Place to Me?", p. 6) and the heart's determination to express, and thus absorb, its "vivid pain" ("The Hours", p. 8). The answers which emerge in the poems are not simple: both the "burning martyr" and the "Mystic Friend" abide there ("Memory", p. 24). Though they mark no clear ascent from the "prison of loneliness and despair" ("In a Far Land", p. 10), the poems do chart their course, with the courage of an unrelenting honesty, through a shadowy terrain where

> The airs are cleft,
> The seas are dry,
> Day is dark
> And night burns . . .

Poised as they are between the mind's recognition of the need for boundless faith and the heart's experience of crippling despair, these lyrics stand as evidence of the power of the human spirit to endure any loss, no matter how great. They are also a testimony to the capacity of faith to transmute the dross of human love into a spiritual bond, enduring, potent, and rare.

Those who claim to understand the mourning process

xiv

tell us that, ultimately, grief must find its full expression. Perhaps, with Shoghi Effendi's mission assured and its achievements throughout the world everywhere manifest, there is at last time for mourning.

Douglas Martin

1. Bahá'u'lláh had appointed His son, 'Abdu'l-Bahá, as head of the movement following His own passing in 1892. It was 'Abdu'l-Bahá who laid the foundations for the organization of the Bahá'í community and conferred on Shoghi Effendi the responsibility of its Guardianship.

2. Rúḥíyyih Rabbani, *The Priceless Pearl* (London: Bahá'í Publishing Trust, 1969), pp. 444–45.

A WASTE, A WASTE THE WORLD TO ME

Which way does the heart turn
To escape from the beat
Of the soft little running feet
Of memory?

Where does one rest the frowning brow
Of the poor dazed prison head
Where every hope and joy lies dead
From a thousand wounds?

What does one do with the minutes,
The hours, the days, the years before
That stretch endlessly beyond the door
Now battered down—

A waste, a waste the world to me
Not wide enough to hold my soul
No refuge, no haven, no goal
In all its space.

Time falls down on my bowed head
Like winter's first thick flakes of snow
And spring again I shall not know
Nor any green.

The blazing crown was laid—
Invisible to all but me—
In his dead hands, for king was he
And went away.

And with him went my every hope
My love, my laughter, all my life—
Unworthy being who was his wife—
All my all.

He was the great pearl of God
Born of the seas that were twain
Such jewel will not be seen again
In this low sphere.

He was the mighty tree of God
The axeman came and struck its root,
The King lies dead and deaf and mute—
And who is King?

A little flutter of the pulse,
On waking up a single sigh—
Is it right the world should die
With one man?

Go your way world, mad as ever—
But for me there is no peace or war
My love, my love is gone forevermore
And left me.

I kissed his brow and took his hands
So beautiful and soft to feel in mine
They curved about my fingers, supine
In death.

I gazed upon his blessed face
And never saw a beauty so sublime—
It was my last look for all time—
In agony and joy.

I laid him in his second shroud
And carpeted his sleeping form with flowers
From Holy Places inmost bowers
A cloak of love.

I tucked the petals in his hands
And laid the soft white silk so warm
Over all his treasured form—
Across his face.

My love I tucked you in for aye
And on your breast a crimson rose—
With what prayer and kiss God knows—
I gently laid.

But why should I be left behind?
Is any sin worthy such banishment?
Lucifer was thus given judgement
And who am I?

Dear love, I told you never
Could I live far from thee;
Dare any ask this sacrifice of me?
God or man?

On the cage-bars of my soul
I beat my fists to bloody shreds
I try and break the subtle threads
Of heart's beat.

I cry out and bang upon the walls
Of my poor bemused tormented brain
I beat and cry, in vain, in vain,
No ear hears—

I have not sinned so much
That God should cast me down so far,
Nor am I saint to rise, a shining star
On this black night.

I am only love, a soul's deep love,
Bereft of all its all struck to dust
Let no man say live now she must
For duty's sake.

How dare they ask this thing of me?
Can a poor plant live without its earth?
Will some man name to me the worth
Of such sacrifice?

2 December 1957

THE BECKONING LADY

You stretched your fair white hand to me
Oh lady of the sun-rays hair
And eyes reflected from the seas
And said, "Come, come, give me your hand."

But I hated you for your name was Life
And your touch was life—
Its fullness.

And through my tears I cursed you
And drew away my hands
And covered my broken heart
And cried, "Never, never!"

But wicked fair one
You sent your dogs to hunt me
And they fell on me behind
While I looked only at your face

And their weight on my back
Is carrying me down,
Their cruel weight.
They are the hounds of duty,
The dogs of other people's desires,
The cruel pursuers
Of the poor bird trembling in the woods.

And if your hounds capture my life,
Think you I will love you
As of yore?

Robber, heartless woman
Who would steal the flower of grief
Out of my trembling breast!

Is there no pity in your muffling,
Exuberant, stifling love?
Do you not know
That love is a jewel beyond your price?

Buy me you may,
But my pearl you shall not have—
I hate you, I hate you,
I hate you.

2 December 1957

WHAT IS TIME AND PLACE TO ME?

What is time and place to me?
I wait in my station
For a train that will never come.
I travel on my train to a station
That never will be reached.
My back is turned to thoughts of day,
A window has opened onto space
And endless, endless night is there—
The stars are a cold light
And do not cheer my heart.

People talk to me of life,
Chattering like geese about a pool
Where duckweed grows midst dragonflies.
My heart is like an eagle,
Soaring, ever soaring higher
Away from the world,
Its valleys, its hills, its plains—
Away, up to the burning blinding sun.
My sun is death.

Will they not know, and if?
Let them know or not,
It changes naught, neither me
Nor my stark horror.

Poor, foolish souls, to them the world
Is still better than eternity—
Or oblivion—whichever it be.
To me the world is bitter dust
To be stamped beneath my feet
As I leap up and away!

4 December 1957

MY HEART TUGS AT ITS WEAK CABLE

Who will hear and who will care
Now you my love are "there"?
The light of the sun is a blight—
Which more heinous, day or night?
Every blooming thing repels my eyes
For my all in all in your grave lies.

They care, but hear they are unable.
My poor heart tugs at its weak cable
As a ship that will away to sea
To you my love, to you I flee!

So apt I told you in my joy
That your love had changed my base alloy
And made it over, something new
Unworthy but melted down in you, in you.

I told you dear, so many times
That I could never tarry here betimes
When you were dead, I too
Would come swiftly, after you.

How have you left me all in chains,
You who solaced all my pains.
How could you leave me here behind—
You ever were so kind, so kind?

Ah, free me from this living hell
Take the poor prisoner from her cell.
Hear her anguish in the night
Pity her weeping, pity her fright
Lift her to your breast again
Heal the wounds, the pain, the pain—

5 December 1957

THE HOURS

Which hours are the worse
The jackal hours
Or the wolf hours?

The jackals are the hours of light
They come laughing and snapping
With the sun—

The wolves are the dark, the dark,
They slink close to me
With their red eyes glowing
And their wet lips slavering
With unappeased hunger.

All day the horror of emptiness
And the anxieties the light brings,
And all night the horror of memory
The haunted chambers of the mind
Where the soul wanders homeless
Touching with feeble hands
A thousand, thousand thoughts!

Like the images in delirium
That expand into giant forms
Comes the poignancy of a re-seen moment—
A lake, the sun on the hills,
A room, a smile, a look, a word.

It rises up like the jinn,
Unsealed from the fisherman's flask,
Until my heart recoils in terror
Before the dagger of feeling
Plunged again and again
Into the self-same wound—

And yet I cannot live
Without this vivid pain—
I cannot bear a scab should ever grow
Over this bleeding wound so deep.

I cannot bear it should hurt me less,
Lest by one infinitesimal grain
The sacred treasure of my love
Should be despoiled in sum.

5 December 1957

WAS IT RIGHT, MY LOVE?

After you died my love,
After you left me here,
The people came and walked
On my heart as a road—

All its poor breaks, carefully hidden,
They trod on day after day—
They did not mean to,
But I wondered if the mud
That stuck to their feet was red?

I was pilloried, my love,
Alone, alone—God knows
I tried to shield you there,
I tried to cover your hurt—

Had we not wept enough?
Had we not sorrowed in vain?
Was it right, you dead,
I left behind alone,
That they should say
Over and over, repeated again,
"He having had no child"?

It rains and it rains,
And my tears fall down
In steady company
And in each tear a world
Of memory hangs reflected
Before it falls on my breast.

7 December 1957

IN A FAR LAND . . .

The rain drops are dancing their mad pace
On the window panes,
Whipped by the lash of the wind
And I am thinking that in a far land
They are dancing on your grave tonight.

Back and forth, back and forth
The merry little grey feet go
In their whirling quadrille
And there as here the big trees bend
Double and sigh and moan.

And there as here the thunder roars
From out the place called heaven
It shakes your home here.
Does it shake your vault there?

It shakes my heart with long shudders
As it shocks my tired ears.
I think it does not shake your heart
There in your cold breast in England.

But the wet earth about you
And the damp blowing leaves
Are not half as forlorn or dreary
As the icy wet cell that confines me
The prison of loneliness and despair.

Where the feet of my mind
Shuffle endlessly back and forth
Remembering what should have been—
What was promised but never given.

Remembering a million loving hopes
Cut back ruthlessly by fate—or God—
As one would trample a butterfly
Drying its wings from the cocoon.

Ask me not why; I am tired of answers,
Tired to the bone of life and of men.
I envy you there in your silent grave
With all the other dead people about
Sleeping or dreaming—who knows?
But at least far from living and life.

Like the beating of many wings
Admonitions fall on me left and right
The wind they raise is called "duty".
Were no duties owing me in life?

My greatest sin was surely this
My faith knew no earthly bounds
It waited as a hollow for dew,
A flower for the morning sun.

Believing God's mercy would surely come,
Believing and believing with each added blow,
Hoping when others laughed at hope,
Saying always, "God is God",
Holding to His miracles of old—

Your hands love are withering in death,
Through mine fall thick my tears.
How much we endured together.
Shall we now endure death apart?

7 December 1957

13

ALL THINGS REMIND ME OF YOU

All things remind me of you,
The rain and the sun,
The treads of the stairs
I came up a bride, long ago,
The pebbles in the paths,
And the streets of many cities,
The steps in your beautiful gardens,
Each flower and rose and tree.

I myself remind me of you,
For your words and your looks
Catch me up in a thousand ways,
Homely, tender ways of daily
Life lived long together.

Like a planet I revolve in my orbit
Around and around and around,
And my centre is my boundless grief,
My insatiable longing for you,
My love that flames all my breast.

9 December 1957

WHY IS THE DOOR OF HEAVEN CLOSED?

A good man had a dream:
Two Holy Souls came out the tomb
And took the high-born scion
Of their glorious and noble house
And entered in the tomb again,
The wall seamed up its sudden gape
And all was still.

Why is the high door of heaven closed?
A Hurricane took the scheme of God
And wrapping it in wings of fire
Hasted through that mighty portal.
Midst the clapping of thunderous waves of air
It locked on men's faces.

Now in all the lands they watch
The cold high gates of Heaven
And like children, with frightened eyes,
Scan for any crack—a chink of light!

As the wheat fields bend and sigh
In mighty summer winds
The hearts of men are lashed;
Thrashing to and fro in agony,
Grief, despair, wild hope, prayers.
Why, God, O Mighty God, why?

In waves this query beats
Upon Thy Kingdom's door
And ever and again the echo
Alone, forlorn, hollow, comes back—
Why?

We are Thy children, Lord!
Have mercy, Pitier of Thralls.
Forgive, heal, stretch forth a hand,
And save us from ourselves.

Else into universal night we slip
Sunk in rings and rings of dark
And all Thy bright day fades
Forever from our hearts, and we
And others, who hoped less,
Go down to everlasting doom.

9 December 1957

THE FUNERAL

Emerald beneath and crimson above
The green of life and the martyr's blood
We spread for thee in our great love.
We bore thee high on a flood of tears
With the sighs of our hearts,
The devotion of all our years.

We could not look upon thy face—
The wound of death to us too deep—
But all felt wrapped within thy grace,
The grace of deeds thou didst do
So patiently, heartbrokenly, so long—
Our father, our guide, our brother true.

We gazed upon thy grave new-made,
A thousand hopes and dreams
Deep with thee in it we laid.
Bent backs, bowed heads, hearts eaten
With remorse at works undone,
Our very souls and minds beaten
Down by conscience, grief and love,
Each asked what part he or she
Shared in this visitation from above.

Thou wert given to us long ago
By One greater than thyself;
Thy worth we never came to know
Until the casket small under the rain
Lay bare before our gaze;
Thyself within never to rise again
And greet us with thy radiant smile,
Thy flashing eyes, thy dimpled cheeks,
Thy voice that could beguile
The hardest heart, the hardest head.

We knew thee not beloved
Till all farewells were said
And each one bowed or placed his kiss,
Not on thy cheek so warm and dear,
But on thy casket—only this.

We knew thee not beloved one
Until thy soul took up its flight,
Thy mortal journey done.
We knew thee not beloved one
Till we strewed thy rooted grave
With sacred flowers, and said, "'Tis done".

Gone from our gaze, our touch—
We mourn deep, deep inside.
What men lose they value much.

12 December 1957

LOFTY MANSIONS

They say your story, love
Should now be written down.
Who could ever read it?
Long ere the first page was done
Tears would eclipse
The dancing words
And any proper heart or mind
Would rebel against the pain.

There are primordial scars
Deep down in Mother Earth,
Traces on her molten heart
Where creation injured her.
The little racing blades of grass
Have covered these over in love
So that no eye need see
The earth's deep hurt.

A veil must cover this too, love.
Your life? It must shine
In works of praise,
In dates and days and names;
The lava bed, now stilled,
That surged through your soul
In white-hot agony
Must be let alone by men,
Their pens are not fitted
To measure the degree
Of your cataclysm.
Nor could paper bear the tale.

Your own tears would rise
Like a torrent-sewn river
And wash away the words
If I ever wrote them down;

My tears would flow,
A strange crystal ink
Spilled over any tally
Of your deep wrongs and pain
And carry the words
Away, back into the sea
Of suffering from whence they came.

No, silence is best,
For after all, there did grow
On the tree of your infinite pain
A gem-bestudded fruit
You made to scintillate,
The lofty mansions
of God's Holy Cause.

You lighted up the lamps,
Made wide the halls for men,
Spread out the costly rugs
And marked the way—
So let it be.
The building blocks were tears,
Heart's blood the lime
That held each stone.
The trowel you used was pain—

But let it be covered deep
In your memory
In my memory—
Let men have their dream palace
They need not know its price.

13 December 1957

THE SHUTTING OF THE DOOR

Many things have been revealed to me
Of the feelings of men in the dawn,
When the world was young and history
Had not yet grown up as now.
I wondered at the Pharaoh's tombs, and all
The trappings buried there, the boats, the slaves,
The jewels, the very food wrapped in dust's pall,
Lying hidden in the hills for ages past.

The Hittites, the Assyrians, Stone Age men too,
Into the grave, great or small, went daily things
I could never grasp the why till one day you
Went into your tomb before my weeping eyes.
Then I knew 'twas love, burning, seething love,
Hotter, simpler than men ever know today
That made them lay in the earth things from above,
Not abiding the dear one should rest so alone—

I think not they thought man's voy'ging soul
Would carry on its way clay vessels;
They knew it sped alone to a higher goal.
But love, o'erpowering reason and grief,
Laid the dear daily things in the tomb
So the beloved one would not appear
So abandoned, so left alone in the gloom,
When that last door was shut in silence.

I used to shudder when as a child
I heard widows were burned on funeral pyres—
They said the Indians were cruel and mad and wild;
Now I see deep reason, a long ago reason,
In what once was keenly, passionately felt.
If love were there, if sorrow knit the ties,
It was not cruel but rather kind to melt
The living clay with the dead clay in flame.

I always hated black and oft have sworn
Never to carry it for loss of those I love;
But when grief rises till all the atoms mourn,
As well as heart and mind—black is the mirror
That depicts the troubled soul, no light
Can reach it when despair folds close
And closer over very essence; it is right
To wear the black badge of Fate's decree.

For me the wheel of many centuries
Has spun about, and suddenly
I am alien to my time
And wrapped deep in doubt
From our ultra-civilized today.
We reason, we are wise, we say
A thousand truths, prove them by writ—
But all I know, for me there is no day,
All is night, dark longing, all in pain—

Those people of old, long ago,
They seemed to fit into life better than we,
They felt, as suddenly I know,
With passionate, deeper, holier feeling.

14 December 1957

WHAT IS THE USE?

Words and tears
And tears and words
And prayers—
Like coloured marbles
Rolling down a hill
They bound about
This house.
And what is the use,
What is the use?

The Spinner no more
Turns the wheel,
The Miller's stone
Is still.

The Garner's hand
Itself is scythed
Off and fallen!
And what is the use,
What is the use?

The symphony
Is still,
The cacophony
Of crickets
Rises in its place.

The Painter's brush
Is fallen,
And upon the palette
Steps the ass.
And what is the use,
What is the use?

Eyes that scanned
Heaven itself
And read there
Designs in airy palaces
Are closed.

Little men bend
Their petty gaze
Upon the ground
Seeking to divine
From the worm
A mystic pattern!
And what is the use,
What is the use?

The airs are cleft,
The seas are dry,
Day is dark
And night burns;

A strange music
Fills my ears,
I dare not
Give it name!
And what is the use,
What is the use?

16 December 1957

AN INVOCATION

There is no other healing for this wound
But earth, and dust
To staunch its flow.
Pour on the gentle soil
In whose every grain life
Adheres a thousand-fold,
Heap it on my heart and head—
There is no other healing for me.

The balsam of life's greatest gift,
Death, majestic, final, seal of seals.
Give me this to staunch my blood
For the wound bleeds endlessly.
I faint, I reel, I fall—
Ah, God have mercy!
Hast thou no ears?
Are they too turned away
Like Thy face
Thou didst show us
In a loved one's face?

Have pity, "Pitier of Thralls"!
Strike off the chains
And set me free.
My whole being thirsts
Like a restless river
For the desert of death!

18 December 1957

I HAVE A RENDEZVOUS WITH DEATH

I have a rendezvous with death—
Sweet death, dear death,
Soon or late I come to thee.

My ancestors were wild folk,
Highland folk, deep, keen,
They plied the sword
For those they loved,
They grinned and parried,
Spilt their blood,
Died for lost causes
Counting not the cost!

The same blood flows in me,
I'll race fate one last course
About the green,
Give destiny a run
For its black money—
And then, my friends,
I have a rendezvous with death—
Dear death, sweet death,
I'll come to thee.

18 December 1957

CLOCKS OF THE SOUL AND MIND

The hours strike slowly—
But not on clocks made by men's hands,
On strange clocks of the soul and mind
Attuned to catastrophe and grief.

A minute is a thousand thoughts,
One painful thought a year,
A month is yesterday's wild pain
And yesterday a lifetime past—

Past, present blend in memory
And memory becomes eternal—
Future twists back like a serpent
And bites the heart
With the black venom of the past—

Each second falls like water,
Wears away the stone of life,
But life burns up like cobwebs
In a sudden blaze.

19 December 1957

MEMORY

I suppose those are stars
Shining in the sky?
That moon really exists?
That those who live lives
Are alive?

To me they are shadows
Passing on a screen,
The screen of my grief,
They flicker in my tears,
Phantom beings going by.

The stars, the moon,
A backdrop
For my stage
And all my heart
Is the stage.

And you, you my love
Are all my theme!
Memory is the play
And ah, what tragedy
It conjures up!

Back and forth
The reality of vanished days
Moves in a Passion Play
More terrible to me
Than martyrs' ways—

And each step
My players take
Pulls all my heart strings
Till I think the case of me
Will surely rend and break—

But no, back and forth,
Back and forth
My mind moves actors,
Scenes and nations
In a daze.

More vivid than nightmare,
Like a vista seen
In lightning's fire,
What once was life to me
Takes on an agonizing form
And love and longing
Speak their lines unendingly.

Where is the key, the cord—
Where that one small knot
That ties the soul
To flesh weary of life?

Ceaselessly the fingers of my will
Feel in my depths,
Feverishly pulling at the bars,
Probing, probing for the switch
That snuffs breath like a candle
In the throat
And leaves the broken heart
Still at last.

It is not right
That God, Nature and Fate
So should anchor man
In flesh's bitter harbour
That he cannot release
His sails and voyage
Over the rim of life
Into the unknown!

It is not right one being,
Poor, weak and undefended,
So should be put upon
That like a timid beast
It cowers in its cage,
Or like a moth upon a pin
Quivers and does not die!

God, dost Thou not see
My joined hands,
My rain of tears,
My eyes going blind in grief?

Creator Who made man in love
Where is Thy love now?
How long must the martyr burn
Before the Mystic Friend
Ransoms him from life?
How long, oh God!
How long!

28 December 1957

OBLIVION

Thy blessed, blessed tree Bahá'u'lláh
Cut down without a trace?
See how the wind with fairy hands
Carries a thousand seeds,
Blown hither and yon
From the purse of God!

All things bloom, beget, burgeon
In Thy never-ending life.
Thy tree, oh Lord,
Without a single seed?

God art Thou cruel or deaf or blind?
My hearts says No, Beloved One,
Thou art all things
And all things from Thee are good!
Then, O my Lord,
Why lies Thy Tree upon the ground
Its mighty crown withered in the grave!

O God, O God!
Pitier of Thralls art Thou,
The "Unconditioned",
And in Thy hands of might,
Hell and heaven's dominion;
Hast Thou no time for me?

In Thy bright fields on high
Grows there no balm
For all my wounds?
O God, O God!
Have mercy, let me die,
Not death of reunion,
For I am too weary for more life,
But death of oblivion.

Let the eternal dark
Fold me in its arms
And earth stop up my mouth.

Since Thy Tree is gone
Without a seed,
Let this empty husk
Vanish in dust,
Heartbroken, unhealed of life's wounds,
Forgotten as time goes by—

                    30 December 1957

GRIEF

As sugar blends with water
Until the two be one,
So grief and love in me
Are blended through.

Can I put from my lips
The burning draught
Of bitterness
Sweetened with all my love?

Can one divide the heart
From its blood
And live on in peace?
Ah no!

Every tender memory
Wrapped about with thorns,
I close upon and seize with pain
And weep as I rejoice!

December 1957

ONE HOUR LESS OF LIFE

I count my rosary of hours
Each bead a part of life
And rejoice for every pearl
Slipped past my feverish grasp—
One hour is gone!
Hosanna to the Lord
One hour less of life!
One day is folded away
In its tears and loneliness
And my tormenter, night,
Much as I hate
His pitiless eyes,
Heralds a new day
Which in desultory turn
Will close and leave me
That much nearer
My eternal sleep.
I watch the clock;
Will the hour never turn?
The hands are fixed
As my brain is fixed
And do not move—
When lo, a month is fled!
Buffeted and tossed
From agony to agony
Like a man caged in a vortex
Who sees now east now west
As he spins to his doom,
I see first thy face
In a thousand forms
And then black destiny
With all its sucking mouths
Like an octopus's arms
Reaching to catch me,

To lash me down,
To bleed me dry!
And where is God in all of this?
Like a summer breeze
That suddenly rises
And ripples over the fields
Ever and again He stirs
Over me in a wave
Of comfort—too soon gone!
What use to tell the cauldron
Boiling on the fire
"Be still, let heaven's image
Come to rest in you."
Put out the flames,
Cool the ravaged heart!
Then peace may find a way—
Who knows?

1 January 1958

LIVE, SAID MY FRIENDS

Live, said my friends,
And I answered, Why?
Live for the lark at dawn
And the moon on soft seas,
For the breeze in the grass
And the warmth of the sun!
For these, said I?

For the cruelty of man
And the heartless word,
For the agony of longing
That wells like fresh blood
From a heart stabbed to the core?

For the endless work
That beats the body
To a heap of dust
Where each atom quivers
Long into the frightening night?
For the emptiness, emptiness, emptiness
Of every single hour?

Live, said my friends,
For we love you well!
Aye, well in your way,
But have you a home,
A love, a child?
Did God give you perchance
Brother, sister, father, mother?

When you look on day
Does it shine bright
To your sleep-fresh eyes,

Or is it an insult
In all its fairness
To the unending woe
In your tortured soul?

Then live for God,
Said my kind friends!
I have lived for God
In my poor way
For nigh half a hundred years,
Weak, erring, frail,
Yet Him I put first
And loved most—

But He has forgotten—
His Almighty Mind
Is turned to other things.
The aging slave
Stands at the door
And weeps in vain!

If God forget me,
Foolish friends,
Shall your remembrance
Staunch my wound?

2 January 1958

CALL ME AWAY

Ah, my love!
When I found you cold
Upon your strange bed
Ask me not
What hand
Was laid upon my heart!

But I buried you, dearest—
Yes, at the last
'Twas I who stood
At head, at feet
And saw you safely
On your way!

'Twas my lips, dear
That kissed your icy brow,
My hands that folded
O'er your tranquil form
The silken shroud—

My hand that laid
The rose upon your breast
And covered your coffin,
Your tomb, your grave!

Ah love, love,
I cannot live away
From you, my all in all!
Break my bonds
And set me free!
Lest I tear them
Myself and flee away
To some dim corner
In some forgotten grave!

In the name of God
Of human pity
Of faithful love,
Call me away!

2 January 1958

BE QUIET MY HEART

Oh still and silent heart!
Do you hear the small voice
That calls from mine to you?
It says with every beat
"Beloved, beloved, beloved",
And every surge of blood
Cries out, as vivid life
Flows in its carmine river,
"Set me free, free, free"!

Be quiet my heart,
Be patient yet awhile,
You do not beat
As steady as before
And ever and anon
A quiver of swift pain
Breaks your timed rhythm—

The pain comes oftener
And each stab of pain
Is like the rays of the sun
Bursting through storm clouds.
On each blade of pain is written "Hope"
And the thrusts comfort my soul
For it thinks it sees
A door opening.

Dear silent heart,
How oft my ear
Was pressed to you
And I listened and counted
The steady beats,
For the life therein
Was the life of the world

And each throb precious
Beyond all counting.
And as I listened
I knew in those beats
Was woven too
A portion—ah sacred gift!
Of love for me!

Dear silent heart,
Empty cup in which
God's own sweet wine
Was once encircled;
Strong heart, courageous
That never flinched
From threatened thrust
But stood bared
To the world's wild blows!

As a magnet
Draws its steel,
A flame its moth,
Draw now my heart
To stillness
Close beside you
In death's gentle comfort.

3 January 1958

LOOSE THE GALLING THONG

The weary head was often bent
Upon the fingers of the hand
And one living member lent
To the other a living touch
And the humbler hand sustained
The brow, life flowing to life,
Inner communion maintained
Of the soul with all its parts.

But yester-eve, I bent my brow,
Weary with living and longing,
On my fingers—and I now
Of a sudden, with what thrill!
Felt beneath the hand a skull
And the fingers were bones,
The skeleton, thin and silver-dull
Gripped my poor forehead!

Ah, peace and promise divine
What healing in mine own touch!
Forecasting this narrow confine
Of flesh might soon be breached!

From bone to bone in mystic flow,
The sweet current of hope
Did surge and throb and flow
And spoke back to the heart
"Hope, poor heart, hope once again
For where God is deaf
Nature will not be called in vain
Her hand will loose the galling thong!"

5 January 1958

42

AH, MY LOVE!

Ah, my love
They tell me
"Dry your tears
And cease to grieve—
'Tis not meet
Before eternity
To lament so long,
So deep"!

They do not see
That all my heart
Cries for you
As if you were
My heart
Torn living
From my breast!
What shall I place
In this gaping wound?

Day is night to me
And night a fierce
Strange day
Blazing with memory.
They think
I mourn you
As a wife
Mourns her
Much-loved mate—

How can I ever
Make them see
This is non-existent!

I mourn you
As the rain
Weeps for its lost cloud,
As the ray
Burns for its lost sun,
As the scent
Faints for its lost flower,
As the echo dies
For its lost voice!

I never knew
Such strength was mine.
Like some strange metal
Forged for outer space
I subsist in the heat
Of utter longing!
But incandescence
Comes at last,
Soon or late
My soul will burn
Away its prison
And be gone.

7 January 1958

THE SECRET

I bowed to Death
And said "Good day,
Will you not stay
With me and dance?"

He grinned and bowed
Deep in his turn,
I thought he does not spurn
My invitation.

But when it came
To set the pace
He did not take his place
But only stared—

"Why do you stare,
Partner?", said I.
"Come, for I would try
A waltz with you."

He looked at me
The longest while
Then said, with a smile,
"I waltz with you
All night and day,
For I am in you.
Through and through,
My fiber's there."

"What! I so full
Of blood and life,
In my heart beats
No strife nor pain!"

"Nevertheless",
Said Death to me,
"I am in you, see
Yourself within!"

I felt as I gazed
Upon my hands
The bare bones
Within the flesh,

And all my length
Was filled with bone,
My skull like a stone
Behind my living face—

"A skeleton am I",
To him I said,
"Long before I'm dead
You are in me!"

He smiled again,
A kindly smile,
"Wait yet awhile
And I shall come

"And call you out
To me, to love, to life
Away from strife,
To fields of peace;

"You shall pick
The daisies there
In those meadows rare,
Each flower a star;

"You shall not fret
Nor grieve and weep—
I promise sleep
To you at last;

"Be patient yet awhile,
See how I grow each day
In you, more deep my sway
Over your life."

The skeleton
Shines like a light
Through the flesh so slight,
Till at last
It burns away
The cage, and free
You'll come to me—
Not yet awhile—

18 January 1958

47

MY HEART

It was broken
Long ago—
How can it ache
So much?

It was torn—
What waters of grief
Can it hold?

From a cloudless sky
How can rain fall,
And in the black
Of frowning heavens
Whence shine
The stars?

But the place
That was
My heart
Aches on,
And the tears
Rain down.

Like a flask
Of rare essence
Dashed into
A thousand pieces,
Scattered.

So my love,
My pain,
My longing,
Rise as perfume

From this
Decimated heart
And fill
All my being—
Ah love!
Does it waft
On thy blessed face?

19 January 1958

WITH A RUSH OF WINGS

Alas, alas,
I'm filled with steel—
God poured into my mould
A hard and boiling metal,
It melted away in a breath
The frailties of the flesh—

The heat of a broken heart
The icy clutch of despair,
The pain of ultimate fatigue,
Fall off this inner core
And leave the frame
Shining in steel—

But withal there cracks
And moves within
The soul seeking
Its own way out.

The best of armour
Has its chinks,
And many a prince
In olden wars
Was probed through
Some crevice in his plate—

My soul will find
That one small spot,
As water finds a way,
And seeping through
Escape its prison
And be off
With a rush of wings.

19 January 1958

50

NOW REST

All the winds of the universe
Sweep around me
In the dust heap of my thoughts,
They stir the ashes of life,
Left and right,
Left and right.

The frail heap blows,
Hopes, dreams, days, years,
Blown about my mind
In sad and wintry chaos!

What will make the wind fall?
Who will raise up from ashes
The glowing image that once was?

What hand will,
Cool and tender,
Come to the fevered brow
And say, "Rest, dear,
'Tis long enough
And sad enough,
Now rest!"

23 February 1958

THE WOUND

I have a wound that will not heal
The blood flows out again, again.
I have a secret in my breast
Compounded all of pain, of pain!

With what tongue shall my soul lament,
And who will to my plaint give ear?
And who will answer me at last?
I have a longing in my heart—and fear—

I have a restlessness inside me deep
Like the moon-pulled stormy sea,
And who has ever quelled a wave?
And who has balm for me?

I have a longing in my heart
As deep and wide and black as hell,
And this abyss no man can fill
Nor love nor hate nor life can swell
My shrivelled being to a new bud.

I have a wound upon my brow
Branded by living flames breathed there;
It burns my brain as priest's high vow
Set seal of old upon each man
Pledged to God's work for aye;
It sears me day and nighttime too,
And from this wound I die.

26 February 1958

A MILLION STARS OF MEMORY

I think death was only made
For those who really love—
The blow skims off a shallow breast,
The wound heals over-quick—

But as the Pacific deeps
The highest mountains to their bosoms
Could enfold in soundless waves,
So the heart full of its love
Can alone bury death in its depths
And cherish it beneath the waters
Of infinite, aching tenderness.

Ah love that has filled my breast
As the sea, the sky, the eternal snows!
As thoughts of you that stud
With a million stars of memory
My soul's burning firmament!

The measure is too full for one poor being!
Break the cup, put out the lamp,
Dash the mind and pierce the heart—
Give one last blow!

28 February 1958

HEART TO SOUL

My heart brought an offering to my soul
Of blood and tears, of sighs and moans,
"Too little", said the soul, "too little to give!"

"Soul", said my heart, "do not be cruel,
This is the essence of my being,
Lacerated, pressed to purple wine
By the Press of Fate or God.
I have no more than this to give."

"Too little", said my soul, "too little,
For a king's gift is greater still
And sumptuous the feast one lays
Before his gaze, supreme and rich
The treasure poured before his sacred door."

"But soul", said I, "see, 'tis my life,
My dreams, my gossamer cherished dreams!
'Tis the fragrance of all my love,
The fabric of all my tender hope,
'Tis me, me I have brought
As offering at your altar high!"

"Too little", said my soul, "too little!"

Ah me, where shall I hide me deep,
In what black pit cover me o'er,
What will cool this malarial heat
That eats my heart and mind away?
What will dress my wounds that bleed,
What hands cup up my broken heart?

1 March 1958

MY ROSARY

I count my rosary of hours
Over and over again:
'Tis the hour of pain
Hour of shame
Hour of flame
Hope in vain
Poisoned rain,
Again and again and again.

Yesterday, today and ever
All my hoped tomorrow
Oceans of sorrow
Gold and base alloy
Phoenix and poor decoy
A thousand hopes I borrow
To heap upon my sorrow,
Yesterday, today, tomorrow!

Day is long and leads nowhere
Night is nightmare trance
Seeking your glance
While memories dance
Upon each aching nerve
Thoughts reel and swerve
From this sword's glance
Memories advance
That give my heart no chance.

From such torment as this
Is madness not the cup
From which we sup?
Who dares look up?
At such a fate?

It is too late—
The ties are cut
The anchor's up—
Drink deep the bitter cup!

1 March 1958

THE WHIRLWIND DANCES ME

The whirlwind stirs the heap of dust
And sweeps it heaven high.
Can God then stir my puny soul
And make of such as I
A sign for aught of good or strength?

Is anything more low than this,
A heap of bone-dry earth
And shall this be a sign of His
Great power and glory here?

I for one believe it not!
But let no man say
Her blessings great she soon forgot—
Ah no, the soil remembers in its dust
That both the moon and sun
Exalted in heaven above
Are made with it of atoms one.

And I remember to my core
That bright being that shone
Upon my lowly soul betimes,
That blessed being now gone!

My heart is filled to overflowing
And yet my heart is empty all,
Its measure broken wide apart—
A measure from the start too small
To hold such grace as this.

And so the whirlwind dances me
Madly upon the barren air.
I know not what is God's decree
I know not peace nor rest,

I only know the wind's wild thunder
That beats me left and right about
And lifts and sweeps me under
In an agonizing maze—

2 March 1958

THE BLACK PALL

At the meeting of the winds
Where the North and South do blow
Where the East and West wind too
Grapple in embrace, my soul did go.

Baffled she stood there
Beat upon from left and right
Harried, rebuffed, immobilized,
Wrapped about in deepest fright.

Every time she tried to see
A new blow cuffed her upheld face
Every time she sought to run
The winds increased their mighty pace.

The sky was closed tight
The homely earth was hard and bare
Upward she could not go
And down was no place there.

She listened to the tempest—
Perhaps God's voice would flow
Down its roaring reaches
And tell her what she sought to know.

Only the shrieking winds gave answer
Only the wordless winds replied
"Ah, would that He, Almighty God,
Had never made me!" she cried.

"Would my unfortunate spark
Had never been struck off his fire,
Would this seed of His high Will
Had ne'er been born to fate so dire!

"Would I had rotted at the root
The day I first saw the light,
Would my heart had never beat
And grown to know grief's bitter plight!"

She tore her breast, her gown, her hair,
She wept aloud, poor woman-soul
At the meeting of the winds,
In the hurricane's black bowl
She stood alone, alone, alone.

If hands were reached out to her there
In her deepest hours of pain
They were too feeble to deter
The lashes of the winds of fate.

Black destiny veiled her soul about
And pinioned her gossamer wings
With the rain of tears and the hail of doubt.

Broken, bleak, forgotten quite
By God and man and all and all—
She stood and wept alone
Shrouded in memory's black pall.

14 March 1958

HAS HEAVEN NO TEARS LEFT?

Storms were made for the crucible
Of the heavens, O Lord!
Storms were made for the reaches
Of the Seven Seas!

Storms were made for the milky ways
Of all Thy vast eternity—
Not, O Lord, for one small heart
To bear like me!

Catastrophe must have a field,
A sweep of hills and plains,
Over the rim of the world
To pour in whistling flames.

Catastrophe was never made
For one small heart to bear,
O Lord, like me, like me!

The ocean fills a thousand shells
And night lights up a million stars—
One poor heart cannot withstand
A measure made for gods to bear,
One poor heart cannot withstand
The brand of this furnace heat!

Where is the rain?
Has heaven no tears left?
Mine own eyes can never quench
This flame, but only fan
To madder heat its burning pain!

16 March 1958

ECHOES

O Lord, are there with you
In your mighty arsenal
Blades brighter and keener than this
With which to pierce us through?
Are there weapons deadlier
To pluck quivering hearts
Out from our breasts?

You say you slay those you love
To victims of this subtle pain.
Where then the *coup de grâce*?
If mercy comes not from above
Where then shall men find rest?

A king's treasure you have spilt
Upon the wretched wanton earth,
Can mere men stained with guilt
Gather up such pearls as these?

Were ants ever seen as fit
To make their heap of diamond dust
That the mean street beggar should sit
Upon the King's own mighty throne!

If a man lose his rose-faced Fair
Can you thrust a hag upon his breast?
And the mother's heart robbed bare
Of first-born who shall fill?

God, You call Yourself Pitier of all,
God of all worlds and this!
My heart is leveled, a ruined city,
What hand shall now build up its gates?

Resurrection you pledged all men
And the day that knows no night!
Ah, through whom and how and when
Will your covenant be kept?

My hand is cut off at the wrist
I staunch its blood in blackest earth
Lest it bleed on at every twist
Of the agonizing stump!

My eyes are blinded with fire
And tears scald the gaping wound,
Where is balm for pain so dire
And where are new eyes to see?

This crucificial barbed dart
That you so cruelly shot
Into the best I gave you—my poor heart—
How long does it take to kill?

This unspeakable poison of grief
That wracks the sinews of my soul
When will you give the nepenthe of relief
When will you tire of my flaming pain?

Echoes, echoes, echoes fading out
Down the corridors of the stars,
Down all eternity my shout
Rumbles and rings and dies away—

Is every stone within your fane
Stuck in the seamless temple
With the lime of endless pain
And the waters of agony?

And, O Mighty God, if this be so
How can the songs therein be sweet
And hearing them You know
Any joy from pain so deep!

16 March 1958

TO WHAT AVAIL ALL THESE?

Letters to God and letters to men
Letters to the north wind and the south
A stream of tears from the eyes
And a stream of words from the mouth—
To what avail all these?

Beating on the heart's iron gate
Beating on the aching brain
Weeping and crying in the night
And who will solace all this pain—
To what avail all these?

Madness in the inmost soul
A forest fire in the heart
And a mind eaten by grief
Each thought a poisoned smart—
To what avail all these?

Feelings surging in and out
With each gasp of the lung
With each scalding racing tear
From the poor heart wrung—
To what avail all these?

A pack of cards on the wind
Blown to hell's farthest pit
A bubble of red foam
On the bitten lip—
To what avail all these?

Flotsam and jetsam on the tide
Of eternity's passive sea,
A little dreaming and feeling,
And back to eternity—
To what avail all these!

Away all your stars!
Away your trailing veils of light!
Begone to oblivion!
Leave me to the night—
To what avail all these?

16 March 1958

THE HEART

There is healing for disease
There is healing for the break
And the tear and the pain,
But for life there is no healing.

For the seed there is the tree
For the egg the bird
For the larvae the frail moth
But for grief no resurrection!

For joy there is consummation
For love soft lips and a word
For madness there are dreams,
But for sorrow no balm!

There is the match's glow
The fireside's tender flame
The gleaming lamp at night,
But for stellar heat no cooling!

There is a word for every ear
A hand for every cradle
A caress for every cheek,
But for the broken heart no hope!

Then wrap it in dark
And in blood and in tears
And bury it deep in the earth
That its wailing may not wake
Those who sleep in the night!

16 March 1958

THE SCHOOL OF HEARTBREAK

In the school of heartbreak
What lessons teach the gods?
The soul to make or unmake,
The forging of sharp swords,

How to crush the weary brain,
How to dash the hopes of heart,
How to fan flame's sparkling pain,
How to unknit the busy mind,

How to roast and baste and sew
The bird of one's inmost self
Till with agony 'tis so aglow
It flies as flame from out the breast!

How to play on a harp of gold
With notes of trembling pain
A thousand tunes of love untold
Till the harp is melted in that fire

And burnt and rent asunder
With the mad, sad music
Of hell's deepest hidden thunder!
And the soul falls down in faint.

How to pour the eyes into the cup
Of vanished dreams, a potion bitter
For the solitary soul to sip and sup
Fed on its own poison keen.

How to caress the throbbing throat
Gently before the axe man's blade
Comes down to drink and gloat
In the running ruby flow of life!

Ah, what do the gods teach
In that rare school on high
Beyond the happy pupil's reach
But made for those who live to die!

16 March 1958

THE PORTION OF FATE

Why hast Thou grafted on one root
Such bitter fruit
O Lord!

Love and longing
Pain and despair
Hope deferred
Anxieties so deep
They haunt the mind
From dream
To dream
In every sleep!

Why hast Thou woven in one frame
Passions too deep to name
O Lord!

Loyalty high
A hasty tongue
Eagerness unwise
Crushing humility
A hasty heart
Too easy hurt
Bound with
A dog's fidelity
Into a small mind's measure
Too much treasure!

O Lord!
Poor quality
And hasty made
The measure breaks
Beneath the weight!

By what standard
Lord so high
Dost Thou portion
Out Thy fate?

17 March 1958

BLIND EYES GAZING IN THE DARK

I said how can I tear them up
These tender things?
Poor foolish child
The paper of the soul
Is torn in twain
The ink of the heart
All spilled away
And you cling
To the shadow?

When night comes down
And the mirrored face
No more is seen,
Why stand with blind eyes
Gazing in the dark?
All is dark—
Break the mirror!

There comes a weariness
Too deep for all eternity
To ever rest away.
There comes a numbness
To the very soul
No waters of joy
Can ever bring alive.

The soul is petrified,
Only the form remains
A dead and senseless shape
Like a tender worm
Being spun into its chrysalis.

Shall I be woven fast
Into the chambers of my own
Abysmal deeps?

Said you a moth would rise
From this unending prison
And fly once more?
And what if winter blight the moth?
No spring can give it life again!

17 March 1958

WILT THOU DENY ME THIS?

Ah God!
For every treasure here on earth
They say Thou hast a thousand
Up on high.

Then God
For every tear men bleed away
From their inmost hearts
Are there with You
Lakes, seas and rivers
Of this dire misery?

For every sigh
That like a pearl
Is born from out some heart
Pried open in pain and grief
Are there not with You
Tempests and storms
As black as all space?

For the haunted thoughts,
The wild hopeless longing,
The sadness that rains
In tropical torrents
From eyes tear-dimmed,
What dream palaces
Are erected in Thy heavens?

Good never flowered
From evil's breast, men say,
Then tell me, Lord,
How can joy
Bloom on the thorn
Of blackest misery,

74

And of the essence of dark
What star can take its form?

Read me Thy riddle
Father of all
For my soul faints
Upon the way
And Thy gates
Are locked upon me
Even as death
Has locked
My love away—

"Thou shalt not question"
Sayeth the Lord.
So be it—
But Thine arms
Thy breast
Thy lips
Upon my hair
Wilt Thou deny
Thine orphan this?

One touch upon my heart
To cool its heat
One word
However faint and far
It echoes to me.
Wilt Thou deny me this?

20 March 1958

HAVE YOU SEEN MY LOVE?

She set out upon the ways
Of the weary world
And wandered far and near.
She sought in secret lanes,
By soft waters and solitary lakes,
The one she thirsted for—
But wide as the world's ways were
There was no reward for her wandering,
Her restless, aching wandering!

"She" was my soul, my own poor heart,
Condemned to death in life as one,
Fevered with grief grown great in love.
She wrung her hands and walked far, wide ways
And to each one on those distant roads
She sought, she asked and questioned
"Have you seen my love go by?"

My love is bright and brave and better
Than the sun himself which shines!
My love so dear, so kingly, kind and high,
My love so wise and well and strong—
Have you not seen my love pass by?

His foot is small and high, and firm his step,
His hand is quick and small and brown and strong,
His eyes are hazel and grey and oh so bright!
And his smile you will never see again . . .

His voice rings in a plaintive tone,
Full of command and secret tears and thoughts—
Oh, say have you not seen my love
Go over the world's rim, pass on just there?
Tell me, tell me which the road he took!

20 March 1958

76

MY SHROUD

I laid away my cloth of gold
Dead hopes fold on fold
Lest any eye behold
This grief untold.

And when my race is run
And when my day is done
Take this fabric heart-spun
Thread of dreams undone

And wrap me gently in
This shroud my hopes did spin
My last, my grave's fine skin
And lay me near my kin.

Kin is he not I know
But still one sacred vow
Knit to God's mighty bough
This graft so low.

Then in peace sublime
Dust joined to dust so fine
So holy his, so worthless mine,
Lay us near for all of time.

21 March 1958

SAY YES, MY LOVE

My breast has become
The bower of the winds
If heart there is therein
Then 'tis the ghost of a heart.

So light and airy
Is this cage that now
The bird of my soul
Sees escape come near.

Soon the bars
Will melt away
As the morning mists
Fade before the sun.

When flesh becomes shadow,
Substance changes into dream
Then will dreams
Become substance once again?

When dust returns to dust
With a glad sigh
And atoms to atoms
Settle in immemorial design
Will the things of my soul
Take shape and strength
And I be with you again?

Ah, say yes, my love,
Then perhaps my soul
Will bide a little longer
In this earthly cage

And I can do for you
Some few things left undone
When death came to us
And took you quite away.

Love, the bars are so thin,
Latch up the door
Or open it for flight—
Bird and cage are
Wholly yours,
Were, and shall ever be!

21 March 1958

I GAVE YOU ALL I HAD, MY LORD

I gave you all that I had, Lord
My life, my heart, my hope—
The first was poor enough I know
The second unworthy through and through
But the third was a kingly gift
For I hoped on you with all my soul!

I have nothing left to give, Lord
Only my poverty, my ruin, my death—
These fragments, too, I give, Lord
Take them if you will, they're Yours.

Or if not worthy still then spurn
Them for the worthlessness they are!
What can man give You, Lord on high?
Have You needs or wants or hopes?

Whatever You take is mercy pure—
I can but offer as a beggar sits
And stretches out his need to the King
With an empty palm and blind eyes.

21 March 1958

CAN A MAN GIVE MORE
THAN HE POSSESSES?

O God Most High!
Three things have I given Thee
Love, loyalty and trying,
In these have I not fallen short.

But Loved One,
How many sins were woven
In my trying
What unworthiness was blended
In every atom of my love
What poor stuff the loyalty
Given with all the heart I had!

But can a man give more
Then he possesses?
Each flower blooms
According to its kind
Each lamp shines
Its own measure of oil.
Would I had been a better make
That the treasure at thy door
Had been of jewels of star-dust sheen!

Like a child that plays
Beside the ocean wide
And gathers its shells and pebbles—
Its little store—
At the meeting of the waves and beach
And brings this offering of baubles
To its mother's lap,
So I have brought to Thee
All I have!

O God, accept it
In Thy grace.
Forgive Thy child
And take her in Thine arms!

6 April 1958

THE FUNERAL PYRE

From the funeral pyre of death
To the pyre of life
Too many flames
Too many names
Too much inner strife!

From the funeral hall
To the fields of the world
The furor of the mind
The heart's tempest so blind
Wings broken and wings unfurled.

From icy winds of deepest death
The secret unreplied
The longing all denied
Out into spring's softest breath.

Swords are forged in
Dazzling heat and icy shower
But the crystal of the heart
Is shattered in each single part
When death and life wrest for power!

6 April 1958

AH, MY BELOVED!

Were the universe all desolation
It would be my heart;
If every star in the firmament
Were a woe and a calamity
They would be my measure!

Ah beloved, how could you leave me
Here alone in this wilderness of pain
Of work and wandering and weariness
Of longing and love and loneliness!
So would I not have treated you—

Or does God turn deaf ears
There on high and say "Leave her
One more, one less, in the night
Weeping and crying aloud,
It matters not!"

Ah, my beloved!

22 May 1958

WHERE ART THOU, BELOVED!

Over and over again
I ask myself
Is everything nothing?
Is gold ether?

Is nightmare dream,
Or dream comes in the depths
Of nightmare's dark?

Ah God! Is mercy
Hell in disguise
Or is hell a bounty?
Who knows—

The waves of feeling clash
Upon the broken mind
And thoughts like roaring foam
Curl in ceaseless breakers
On a tortured brain.

What does one do
With the pieces of life
Shattered to a thousand bits?
They lie upon the ground,
And each piece aches
And cries out for itself
And all is pain and chaos!

Love is no remedy
For love is all longing;
And faith does not heal
For faith lies bleeding
From a wound too deep
For words!

Poor cells of life
Too strong to die,
Poor spirit too torn
To coalesce and live again!
From which cup
Shall the living dead drink,
On what stone the weary head
Lay its fevered, tortured brow?

The day is a wall
The night is a wall
Each hour a lash
Each day a journey
Never ending, endless in woe!
All winds cry with one voice
Where art thou, beloved!

5 June 1958

MY REST

Three hounds have hunted me
Love, sorrow, and love again
Three suns have shone on me
The sun of spring, winter and summer's flame.
Were they all loosed by the same Hunter?
Were they all kindled at one Fire?

Ask no more riddles in this world
My heart is crucified with pain
My soul's feelings wildly hurled
Cry out to God in vain!
So much life was never given
To one frail mouth to drink!

Then come oblivion with sleep
And take me to your breast
And let the warm earth fold me deep
And let me find at length my rest!

25 June 1958

THE BREAKERS

My soul do you hear that rustling?
'Tis the wings of the night
Gathering with motions of power and of might;

All heaven is filled with the sound,
Like one superb, intoxicating song,
'Tis the wings of life whispering along

The east wind and the north;
'Tis the wings of darkest death
Coming on the south and west winds' breath!

My soul do you hear that thunder?
'Tis the sound of the endless sea
The sea of love that washes me.

The waves roll in from death and life
Each more passionate and each more wild
Till wave on shattering wave is piled
Upon the beaches of my heart
And the poor bleeding shore
Cries "I can bear no more!"

25 June 1958

NIGHTMARE

Nightmare, and who shall find it dream?
Shadows on life's fire-lit screen
They flit and bow and kneel to pray
And kiss and part and fade away
And all is dark and cold and spinning
And there is no end and no beginning—

Nightmare, is dream contained therein?
When the sleepers sleep is thin
He thinks he sees a meaning hid
Beyond the tear-sealed weary lid.
When the sleeper's sleep is deep
He can only moan and weep—

Nightmare, that shudders all the soul,
Has no meaning, hope or goal,
Tossed and struggling, full of pain
The sleeper seeks to wake in vain!
Pity the racked head and heart
That fumbles life from dream to part,

The fingers feverishly picking
Every feeling, like flames licking
Every sense and every thought
Would it could be turned to nought!

Would oblivion could be won
As sleep comes down when day is done,
As death comes down to rest at last
And seals in dust the tortured past!

Nightmare of memories that throng
The halls of mind and fill with song—

Or better, bitter dirge of woe—
Every moments 'membered glow,
Where sun and light and joy
Are stained with darkest death's alloy
And the fugitive spirit reels
From the future mind reveals!

Nightmare of passions warring
And the blood forever roaring
In the weary, bludgeoned head
And the tears themselves weep red

From the wounded heart so still
And the brain a churning mill
That spews from an inner urge
Ideas that seethe and surge
Like a pent-up, restless sea
Whose waves break endlessly!

Nightmare, can one dream in it
As moonlight above storm may sit
And cast a silvern, peaceful glance
O'er all the pangs of sorrow's trance?

Is there an opiate for this pain,
A balsam to make horror wane
In iron reality, a respite fair?
Ah soul, hope if you dare!

9 July 1958

THE PUPPETS

He pulls the cord
And puppets dance
Their eyes are painted
In fixed trance

Their feet beat out
In gestures wild
Their skirts flare out
In gestures mild

Or mad as the puppeteer
Deems fit to pull
The invisible strings
Their breasts are full

Of wooden woes
Their lips are still
The audience laughs
And has its fill!

He pulls the cord
The puppets mime
A play of life
Howe'er He deem

The play is fit
They move their part
Without head
Without heart.

He pulls the cord
And sometimes woe
The creatures quiver
And seem to know

They are but puppets
On a string
A player's sorry
Jesting thing!

He pulls the cord
The wood bleeds
As music comes
From out reeds

Heartbroken music
Piped by blind lips
The puppets faint
The cord slips!

The scene is done
And dull the day
When God made puppets
Dance life's way!

9 August 1958

LIFT ME UP

Heal me in the waters of Thy love
For I am broken, frozen, burnt through—
Ah God, take me to You!

When the heart is split in pain
And the brain drained all away—
Ah God, have your own way!

But in the end give pity,
Give quarter, give grace,
Kiss the dust-stained face,
The tear-drowned eyes.
And breathe Your breath
Into the nostrils
Filled with death!

Are You not Lord?
Can any man deny
By You we live, we die?

Take Your petty world away—
Treadmill of men and strife—
Give me true life
Life of my soul
Where Your nearness is felt
The love the soul does melt

In ecstasy at sight of Your face
At sound of Your voice near
That stills the deadly fear
Of loneliness, of wondering,
Of confusion at Your ways.

Of horror before the days
That lie ahead unknown
The road still to be trod
By feet weary, blood-shod!

Ah God, 'tis only you I want,
'Twas ever You and You alone—
All other loves are flown—
Life, death, world, night, day,
Are shadow things that flee
Your love alone for me!

If my seed was sewn by You
If I grew and lived and strove
It was in the light of Your love.
If I die now, whilst alive
My death will be in You
For my whole being cries through and through

"Lift me up, my Lord, my Life
Lift me to Your breast above
You alone are all my love!"

14 August 1958

WHO MEASURES?

Who sets the portion of tears
Who measures the cup?
Why should seas
Of heart's blood
Be the measure of some?

Why infinite bitterness
Be the stars unnumbered
Of some souls' heaven?
Why are some roads all stones?
Why the crown all thorns?

Why talk to me of blessings—
Was not each bounty bought
At price too high
For even king to pay?

Is the godly one's way
All sorrow and pain?
Is the reward of fidelity
All flames that burn
Until the substance glows
One living, burning column of fire!
Who sets the portion,
Who makes the potion?

Men say life is a balance fine
That all things fit a pattern
A symmetry divine
Set up by God
Called nature.

But ah, 'tis not so!
For some pains
Are so deep, so sharp, so full,
There is no counterpart
Of joy and grace.

Some dark blots out
All light and hope,
Some blows bludgeon
The very soul to dust
Until it drowns in tears

And like a stone
Sinks deep into grief's pool
And only endless rings
Spread out to mark
Its death-place and woe!

17 August 1958

HEAR MY POOR SOUL'S CRY

O God, I sink, I die—
Do you hear my cry?
The weight on mind too great
The weight too heavy
Of Your fate,
Tears are wept dry
I sink, my Lord, I die!

Life is too full, too fast,
Future too soon slips past
And memory tortures every cell
In a separate singing hell!
You do not hear my cry
I fail, I fall, I die!

Yet death comes not to me,
You do not set me free,
And if you did, beyond that door
Wait tears and torture more?

You have ordered men to try
Then hear their piercing cry
And send some aid to heal
Some aid the senses feel

When reeling, spinning seems the world
And the soul's wings are furled
In bitterness, despair and gloom
And all one sees is doom

And darkness on every side,
And no turning of the tide
Of the heart's mad surging sea—
Dost Thou not hear my plea?

O God, have pity, stretch Your hand
And loose the galling band
That bites deep in mind and heart
Remove despair's barbéd dart

Give oblivion and the rest
Of unconsciousness so blest.
I fall, my God, I die
Hear my poor soul's cry!

20 August 1958

ASK NOT WHY

Does one do
One's account with Thee, O God,
A mite and the Sun?

Then I would write
I'm quit of all things.
Let not Thee, or man,
Or him I love above all,
Subtract or add
To this my sum.

I lived, I tried, I bled,
I was weak all way,
I fell but I rose
And tried again
And again and again.

Let no one ask me why
Or say she did thus
She should do so.

There comes a nakedness
When only bone is left,
When all substance
Is burned away.
Only the flame is left.

If it ascend in light,
If it dissolve in smoke,
Let no one question
For we are quits
And I am free.

Forgive me if Thou canst
Or squeeze this heart
Till nought remains.
Thou art God
I only a mite,
But the mite has had its fill
And dares to write
"Peace, leave it be
And ask not why."

22 August 1958

QUAN YIN

When the stars fade in the sky,
When my tears are all wept dry
I go in the dark—Quan Yin and I.
Goddess of mercy, do you hear?
Does your spirit lend its ear
To a mortal tale so drear?

When ruin stretches far and wide,
When my weary head I hide,
Can I on your breast abide?
Mother of Mercy, peace and good
My bleeding heart—Ah, would
My wound your gentle balm
Could reach down and softly heal

With some spirit I could feel
My warring passions to anneal
In a fire divine of love and calm
Give, ah, give some holy balm
To still the brain's mad qualm!

Would in the dark, the lovely deep,
I could feel you hear and weep
Pour out my secrets, you to keep
The painful treasure in your hands!

What paths my soul treads in lost lands
What chains it wears of galling bands!
When the stars fade in the sky
When my tears are all wept dry
Quan Yin, do you hear my cry?

30 September 1958

WEEP NOT FOR ONE BROKEN HEART

There are so many stars!
Weep not for the moon
If it falls in opal dust
Upon the Milky Way.

There are so many worlds!
Weep not for this dusty sphere
If it burns away in the heat
Of some celestial holocaust.

The fence of the universe
Is the fence of all eternity
Weep not for one broken heart
Nor grieve for a passing day!

25 November 1958

ASK ME NO QUESTIONS

Ask me no questions!
Some have too much of life—
Ask me no questions!

The seas, the clouds, the hills, the stars,
Far and vast, mighty and solitary,
Room for the soul but no room at all;
For the heart holds seas far vaster
And the brain is lit by multiple stars
And who can climb the hills of longing?

Ask me no questions!
You do not question the passing cloud
Or meteor that flashes on its way—
Light and homeless as a cloud
Bright and burning as a meteor
Am I, and no home have or rest.

Then ask me no questions,
Leave me before the silent door of death,
Leave me in life's sheath of flame,
And ask me no questions.

4 December 1958

THE BEGGAR'S CUP

There are so many rooms in the house of life,
Dark chambers of the heart and mind,
Where the soul wanders, weeping and blind
Crying for light in the night,
Torn by deepest inner strife.

Right and wrong are easy and clear
When one is young and life's way
Seems spelled out clear as day
And hope flies high
In youth's deep sky
And each month is a blessed year.

But then comes grief and test and flame
And weariness to the very bone,
And fear of all, and being alone.
All is torture dire
All is kindled fire
Shadows that shift without name.

With death then seal the end
With peace and hope and love—
Will the soul soar up above
The broken clay
In heaven's day
Ah, would to will our purposes would bend!

Weary, dragging every step of the way,
Wings cut back to bleeding flags,
Clothed in life's tattered rags,
A beggar's cup
To God held up,
A heart so broken it cannot pray!

7 December 1958

THE MASTER OF THE HUNT IS GONE

The master of the Hunt is gone
With coat of red and shining boots,
With steed that leapt the hedges high
And coattails flying in autumn breeze.

No more the bugle clear and sweet
Sounds o'er the rolling frosted hills
No flashing eye descries the prey
And breakneck pace leads on
O'er every dale and bar and brook!

Only the hounds remain
Wagging their tails and sniffing dirt
Looking once to sky and once to earth
Each thinking in his puny brain
He's fit to lead his master's hunt!

The silver notes are still and still the smile
And rotted in the soil those eyes
Of hazel hue that changed to grey
And gazed with eagerness and fire
With love and hope and brilliant brain
Upon the fellow huntsmen
And the milling, wagging pack.

All things pass,
Pass and are lost in dust,
Or shame or fame—
The Huntsman passed
And only the hounds remain.

15 December 1958

THE PRICELESS PEARL

So many pearls
And so many seas—
But the Pearl of Great Price
Slipped back to the sea
Leaving us desolate on the shore.

So many suns
And so many worlds—
But the sun of our world
Rolled off into night
And left us weeping
In the dark.

The prince without jewel,
The earth without light!
Why profer us pebbles
Or baubles of tin,
Or stars of dim sheen
Or meteors soon gone?

Give back my heart
Its glowing lustrous pearl!
Turn back the clock of days
And light the world
With its own sun
Once more!

Words, words, words—
The mind fingers them
A thousand fold
And drops them at last,
Understanding worn away.

It is the heart
That like a hungry mouth
Cries out for the breast
It once did know,
The very life it sucked.

Why hast Thou drawn
A curtain o'er Thy Face, O Lord,
And veiled from us our love
And taken from before our eyes
Their solace, their deep-won delight?

Sayest Thou "I am angry
And weary of men,
A race of snails at best
That creep upon their slimy way
Timid, slow and fat with greed.

"Suns I gave them,
Moon and star—
And promise of sons
To that most luminous star,
In vain, their sotted eyes
Never raised above the dust.

"They gamboled on the shore
And not one ventured
Within the foaming sea
That lapped their very feet.

"Why should I give my Scion
To strive and suffer in agony
For such shadow beings as these
Who see nor hear nor speak
Nor want the truth!"

My head bows down,
Too broken to speak
Too dry to weep
It only aches on
And on and on—

18 March 1959

FLY, MY LOVE, FLY!

The trees grow higher in thy garden
But thou art gone!
The grass in spring spreads all in green
But their sun is gone!

The faces of the flowers are gay
But the fragrance of the world is gone!
Where art thou, O love,
Where!

The stature of all things has grown small
And the spirits that reached up
Have shrunk back to lowly form,
Thy power that lifted up
The hearts of men is gone!

Ah wilderness of life, my love is gone!
Sun, moon, stars, beauty itself
All, all have lost their charm,
The world is bleak, my love
Because thou, its eye, hast gone!

Dost thou tread other fields
And drink in other joys?
There on high are hallelujahs sung
And cymbals in ecstasy
Clashed sweetly together at dawn?

Does the dew come in peace
And dost thy heart rejoice?
Ah may it be so, my love,
May it be so!

Thou didst take all good with thee
When thou didst go away
May it comfort thy dear heart
In realms far from this world of men!

The bitterness is mine, my love,
May all the splendour of heaven
Shine in happiness on thee!
Forget this dark planet
Veiled in sin and sorrow—
Ah, fly my love, fly!

3 April 1959

THE PILLAR OF FIRE

You came into the world
Like a twisting pillar of fire,
A rumbling and thundering,
A mighty sheet of flame.

We were awed and puzzled
That God and King
And voice from on high
And man here below
Could all be wove into one,
A scion of the Prophet's House
With sceptre and globe
On the throne of man.

Our little hearts rebelled
And trembled and swelled up;
Our little minds fumbled
At the locks of so much mystery.

But in the end we saw,
We saw and gave ourselves to you,
Not a little, not a lot,
But all in all in perfect love.

You became the light of our eyes
The hope of our souls
The solace of our poor minds.
We leaned on you boy and man
As a child puts its brow
On its mother's breast
And knows all will be well.

Ah, where is our pillar of fire!
The roar and the light

111

Are gone over the far horizon
And a sparkle in the sky remains
And a trembling in the earth remains!

We stretch our hands to God,
Older, frailer hands that shake,
And ask "Where is our King?
Why did You give him to us
And why did You take him from us?

"Was our sin so great,
Was Your jealousy so keen,
That the Radiant One
Was called away
From the home of man
Back to Your Kingdom on high?"

The tears fall down
And the words pour out—
To no avail, no avail, no avail!
He came and he went—
One little world, a tiny jot
On a balance sheet
That reaches from eternity to eternity.

Why should He care so much
For us, crawling things
Who did not even know
The fire was here to lose,
To keep, perchance forever?

And so man's life goes on
Well ordered in the light of day,
'Tis white and clean and neat
This day He left with us—

But where is our beloved?
Where the sound of his voice,
The smile of his lips,
The flash of his eye,
The touch of his hand
On pen, on earth, on heart,
On our lives and hopes and prayers!

Red and gold and opal,
Scintillating and warm—
A fire to warm us through
Was our pillar of fire!

When we gazed upon it,
We were won and awed,
When far away
We heard it rumbling
As it twisted and turned
And roared in the world of men.

We laid our heads down in peace
And slept like children at night
Because he was there,
Always there, our new-born King.

God, do you mock us and laugh?
We have no say;
We are unworthy to the bone
And can read our lesson
Vaguely as a child suspects
The end of the world
Is due to some small sin.

Our heads are bent
We weep and grieve
But our pillar of fire
Will come no more!

All the tears in the world
Will but create a sea
Beating on life's shore,
But fire comes from above
And burning out ascends
In rose and incense
To its parent Sun.

6 March 1966

IMAGES

Poor captive in your cage of words
Hemmed in by mem'ries all aflame
Prisoner of fate and self and life—
Ah, seek not to give it name!

You press on the dream bars and peer
Out on the flood of the days and the years
Gone by in storm and in peace,
Washed by too many tears.

I look at your face—poor you—
A shadow of that long ago
When you came, a bird from afar,
A bride, timid and loving, your heart aglow.

Words, too many to push about
Make a pattern none can see
Of days and years gone by,
Into the past, no future to be.

Not in a pool this face reflects,
But in a foggy mirror,
Ghostly you gaze back at me, smiling,
Was this the one who should be Queen?

16 June 1966